DAY TRADING FOREX WITH S&R ZONES

FOREX TRADING SYSTEM

By LAURENTIU DAMIR

TABLE OF CONTENTS

First of all, let me just clarify one thing. The "50 pips" you see in the title on the book is to be taken as an average. It does not suggest or guaranty that you will make 50 pips per day, every day. You will make roughly 50 pips per day, on average. Some days you will make nothing, some days you will make way more than just 50 pips.

On average, at the end of the month, you will find that you have come close to this goal, that the following material tries to accomplish.

Before you start to construct your trading system, you must first think about what is the trading style that suits you better.

Do you want to sit in front of the computer the whole day entering and closing trades on the 5 minute time frame or do you think that trading on a higher time frame will suit you better?

My advice to you is very simple and clear: always seek to trade on the higher time frames. It is easier to trade this way and it will make you much more money in the long term. If you are a beginner in trading, it is best for you not to day trade until you gain experience.

Trading on small time frames carries high risk due to short-term random moves that are almost impossible to predict. Not to mention that trading this way makes you vulnerable against economic news events that come out multiple times per day and usually have a big impact on the small timeframes.

Even after you get more experienced by trading successfully on the higher time frames and you think you are ready to day trade, my advice is to not trade on any interval smaller than the 30 minutes.

Moreover, if you do decide to day trade, consider it as a backup trading style, day trade only when there are no trade setups as per your system on the higher time frames. Always seek to trade on the higher time frame. Nevertheless, as I said before, if you are a beginner trader, and you probably are, I strongly recommend that you develop your trading system around a higher time frame like the 4 hours or the daily.

Forget about day trading for a while. Build your trading system and trade on the 4h/daily charts until you start to add to your account consistently.

COMPONENTS

With the above in mind, the next thing you should decide is what you will include in your trading system from the technical point of view to help you win as many trades as possible. Decide what will be the core technical parts of your trading system.

From my experience, I can tell you which are the tools that work best in forex trading, with a great rate of success. These are price trends, support and resistance levels, Fibonacci ratios, price patterns and bar patterns/candlestick patterns.

These are the things you should consider including in your system. They are the most popular things in the forex market thus, they have the highest rate of success.

PRICE TRENDS

You surely know what a trend is. You see them on your charts every day. The trend is a core principle of the forex market or any market for that matter and should always be considered when constructing your trading system. It is always easier to trade with the trend than against it.

A trend signifies that the majority of traders decided to push the price in one direction.

You must always know what that direction is and trade in line with it.

If you want to know everything there is to know about forex trends, how to spot them by reading the price action, how to recognize when the trend is changing without the help of any technical indicators, you can check out the book Follow Price Action Trends that explains this in great detail, with many chart illustrations, and puts it together into a complete forex price action trading system that can yield thousands of pips by trading these changes in trend.

SUPPORT AND RESISTANCE

Support and resistance levels are also a key component of the forex market; a large number of traders out there highlight them on their charts and base their trading decisions on them.

Therefore, it is advisable that when you decide to construct your trading system you take them into account.

FIBONACCI RETRACEMENTS

Fibonacci ratios are another forex tool that works extremely well in the forex market.

Just pull up any chart and draw your Fibonacci levels from the start to the end of any big move in one direction or another.

You will see how many times these levels act as strong support and resistance zones where price bounces back to resume the previous trend.

PATTERNS

Price patterns and candlestick patterns are also very popular with the vast majority of traders therefore, they too have a great rate of success.

Price patterns are used as signals that price is preparing for a move in a direction and candlestick patterns are used mainly as a confirmation when entering a trade. If you want to learn in great detail about all of these above powerful trading tools and master them, you can take a look at the Trade the Price Action book that explains them very well with many chart illustrations and puts them together in the form of an extremely powerful price action trading system. In conclusion, these are the things that you should include in your trading system because there are by far the most successful tools to trade the forex market. It is completely up to you to decide if you combine them all in your system or just use some of them.

There will be more about these powerful tools in a later section where you will learn how to avoid making trading mistakes when working with them.

NO TECHNICAL INDICATORS

Now that you have an idea of what would be best to include in your trading system you also must know what not to include in it.

Do not use any technical indicators in your trading because they are worthless, they will lose you money overall. You might win a trade today using them but you will surely lose all that money back and more by the end of the week. You should consider yourself very lucky if during one month you manage to break even by trading with indicators.

All indicators are based on past price action, the macd, rsi, or stochastic are not leading indicators. They are only leading you to losses. Being constructed of past price action they are all lagging. By design they follow the past price action, therefore, even if the signals they give would be accurate they are useless because they come too late for you to capitalize on them.

Always remember one thing: price leads the indicator, not the other way around. Do not be fooled when you do a back test on your charts and you see that using an indicator or a trading system with indicators would have made you thousands of pips.

That is just a trick. Real time trading has nothing to do with back testing. When you put that indicator to work in real time, you will soon see that you are wasting your time and money.

Always remember that price tells the indicator what to do not vice versa. The ultimate indicator is and always will be the price action itself. You should focus only on reading and interpreting the price action movements and not overcomplicate your trading system with useless indicators.

200 EMA

From my experience, this moving average is the only indicator that is worth incorporating in your trading system. It is the most important moving average of them all, all retail and professional traders keep an eye on it therefore price tends to bounce when it touches it.

However, it is best to use it in your trading system as

guidance, as a confirmation of what price action tells you and not as a tool to base trading decisions on.

For example, if your system is designed for the 4h chart, you will want to read the price action on that chart to know what the trend is. After you do that and see that the current trend is up or down, you can then look at the 200 EMA on the same chart to confirm and enforce your price action reading.

Let us say the price action trend on that chart is up. If that specific forex pair trades above the 200 EMA at that time on the same chart then you have a confirmation of your price action reading.

You can check out the Trade the Momentum book for a complete trading system that uses this moving average along with some other powerful concepts of trading to make 200 pips per week or more.

Let us see a chart with this moving average so you can

better understand how price reacts to it.

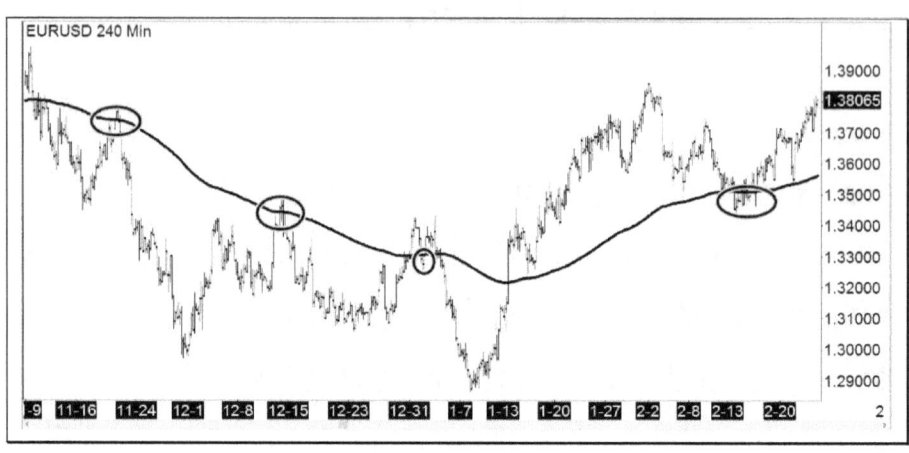

THE 4 HOURS AND DAILY TREND

A good trading system is the one that always refers to bigger picture. The bigger picture in forex is represented by the trends on the higher timeframes.

These trends control the price movement on the lower timeframes. If you design for yourself a system that trades on the 4h charts, you must always take into account the trend on the daily chart. If you trade on the 1h or 30minutes charts, you must always consider the trend on the 4h chart.

For the trend on the daily chart you can use the 200 EMA

discussed earlier. If the pair is trading above the 200EMA on the daily chart, it means that the trend is up on the daily chart. If the pair trades below the 200EMA on the daily chart, it means that the trend is down on the daily chart.

Therefore, any trades entered on the 4h chart according to your trading system should only be entered in line with the daily trend.

This is the way by which you can avoid severe losses and achieve long-term success. Let me show you a trade setup on the 4h chart generated by my Follow Price Action Trends trading system:

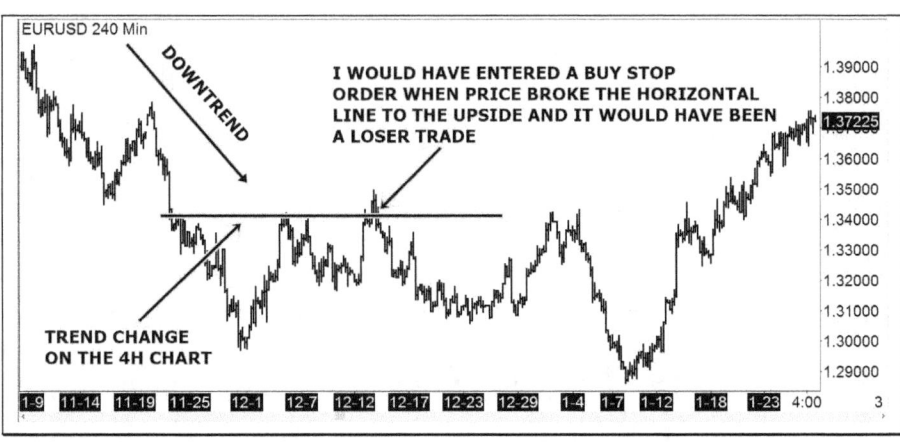

In the 4h chart above, a trade setup took place according to my trading system at that level where the trend changed from downtrend to uptrend on the 4h chart. I should have bought this pair at that circle in the chart.

Well, you can clearly see that price would have gone for a while in my favor only to retrace back down later eating all my gains and hitting my stop loss level. Is the trading system not good? The trading system is very good because it keeps me out of losing trades like this one. It always takes into account the daily trend. And the daily trend for that pair at that moment was:

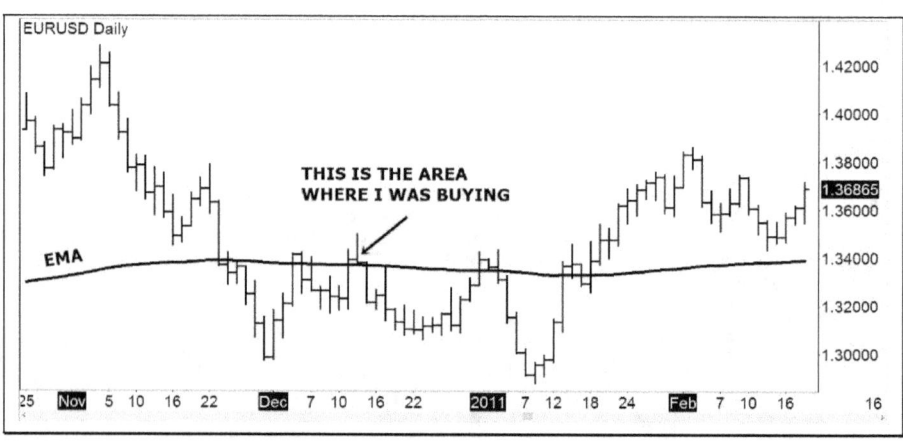

Well, the daily trend was clearly neutral at the moment when I was supposed to enter the buy order. The price action for that pair at that moment was below the 200EMA on the daily. You can see how price just touched the 200 EMA on the daily chart, creeped above it for a very short time period and bounced back down. As per my trading system, I would have taken this trade only if the pair had been trading above the 200EMA on the daily chart.

My trading system kept me out of this losing trade because it always looks at the bigger picture, yours should do the same. When you get more experienced and you want to start trading on a lower timeframe like the 1-hour or the 30 minutes the bigger picture in this case will always be the 4h trend. However, I do not recommend you to grasp the 4h timeframe trend just by looking at the 200 EMA.

The moving average works best to find the trend on the daily chart, for the trend on the 4h chart you will have to read the price action in order to get the best results possible out of your trading. You must determine the trend on the 4h chart by reading the price action, the moving average is not that correct on this timeframe and it can lead you to losses.

The smaller the timeframe, the less accurate the 200 EMA becomes.

The <u>Follow Price Action Trends</u> trading system teaches you with great detail how to spot price action trends on the 4h charts. In addition, the <u>Day Trading Forex with Price Patterns</u> trading system does a great job teaching how to correctly establish the price action trend on the 4h charts but with a different approach.

SOLID MONEY MANAGEMENT

The technical part of your system discussed earlier only solves half of the problem. The other half and equally important is represented by the money management component.

A very good money management technique gives you the opportunity to be extremely profitable with your system even if let us say, out of ten trades, five are losers.

Of course, if you build your system respecting all the rules above and the rules that will follow you won't be in this situation. If, for any reason you should find yourself in it, strict money management rules will make you profitable even in situations like this one.

POSITION SIZING

This is the first rule of money management.

For your system to be a good one, it must tell you how much money you are going to lose on a trade before you enter the trade in the market. To achieve this, you must first have a chat with yourself and think about what percentage of your equity you are willing to risk on a trade. My advice is do not risk more than 2-3% per trade.

Next, your trading system should give you the exact levels where you will enter the trade and where you will place the stop loss level before you enter the trade. Let us do the following exercise:

You have 1000$ in your trading account and you decided that you will only risk 2% of your money per one trade. This means that for the next trade you should risk losing only 20$.

Now, when a trade setup begins to take shape, you decide where you will enter the trade and where you will set the stop loss according to your trading system.

Let us say that you find out you will have a stop loss of 50 pips for this trade. This means that if the trade goes wrong and your stop loss is hit you should lose only 20$. You then divide 20$ / 50 pips to see the value in dollars for every pip that you lose. And that value is 0.4$.

This means that for every pip that goes against you towards your stop loss you should lose only 0.4$. Only after you have this value you determine your order size, which is a simple thing to do since now you know the pip value.

This means you will have to trade with an order size of 0.04 lots (4000$). If you lose the trade: 50 pip stop loss multiplied by 0.4$ per pip equals 20$. You have to do this every time when preparing to enter a trade, always determine your order size this way, manage your risk, always put the bad scenario in front no matter how promising and rewarding the potential trade looks.

Don't you ever think about how much money you could win on that one trade. This will make you emotional, it will cloud your judgment, and you will be tempted to enter with a big order size to win more money out of the trade. Instead, always think of how much money you could lose and do the math explained earlier to determine the size of your order.

RISK-REWARD RATIO

Your system should spot trade setups where the reward is at least 2 times bigger than the risk for every trade.

This means that apart from the entry and stop loss levels, your trading system should tell you the take profit level also. You should know before entering the trade what is the risk and what is the reward.

If your system gives you trades where the reward is not 2 times greater than the risk or worse, the reward is smaller than the risk for every trade then it is not a good trading system.

You will lose your money in the long term. Whenever your system presents you a trade like this, do not take it, no matter how promising it looks. Let us do another exercise to see how easy it is to be profitable if you have a good system with solid money management rules: you have a system that gives you trades with 1:3 risk-reward ratio or more. This means that for every pip you risk losing, the reward is 3 times greater. If you enter a trade with 50 pips stop loss this means that your profit target is 150 pips.

Let us say that on a given month you made 15 trades according to your system, each of them with a 50 pips stop loss and 150 pips profit target. But, the market went crazy that month and out of those 15 trades only 5 of them were winners. 10 were losers.

Therefore, you have only managed a 33% success rates with your trading system, which is very low. Here is where money management shows its value.

Let us do the math. You lost 10 trades with 50 pips stop loss on each of them. This means you lost a total of 500 pips that month. You only won five trades.

With the profit target being 3 times greater than the risk, that is 150 pips won per every trade, this means you have won a total of 750 pips on that month. Therefore, you have lost 10 trades out of 15 which is dreadful but you've still made a profit of 250 pips on that month thanks to money management rules.

STOP LOSS PLACEMENT

Your stop loss should exist for every trade, but the stop loss must always be set at logical places in the market, not randomly. My advice to you is to always put your stop loss at the level where the price has very little chance to reach given the conditions of the market at that moment.

Let us see an example:

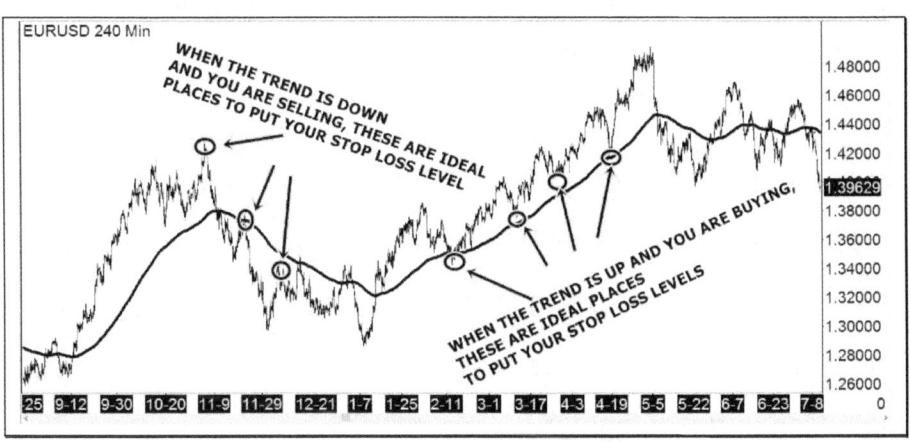

As you can see, when you sell, you put your stop loss just

above the swing highs that price makes. When you buy, you put your stop loss just below the swing lows that price makes on its way up.

If at the time your trading system gives you a potential trade you do not see a logical point in the market like these in the chart above, you do not enter the trade no matter how lucrative it might appear.

PATIENCE, NO EMOTIONS, NO OUTSIDE INFLUENCE

This does not have much to do with money management but it is very important and it has to be outlined. Without patience when trading in the forex market, you have only small chances of success.

If you construct yourself a trading system and 2 or 3 days go by without a trade setup you have to be patient, the setup will come, don't start to bend the rules and chase trades, there is no rule that says you have to trade every single day in order to make money.

Forex is about patiently waiting for the market to present

to you the perfect conditions for a winner trade.

Respect your trading system and trade only by its rules, the trades will come.

Do not be emotional when trading, leave your emotions at the door, and do exactly as the system tells you to do. If your system tells you that you have to trail manually the stop loss above every swing high but the trade has already gone 100 pips in your favor and did not make any swing high yet, wait.

Leave your stop loss at its original place; do not think emotionally, that you have to secure those 100 pips so you do not lose them. This makes you lose money. Completely disregard any comments from individuals on forex forums that tell you to buy or sell because they have the holy grail and they know better than you what is about to happen.

Only trade what your system tells you to trade, do not let yourself be influenced by anyone, no matter how convincing they sound. If you pay attention to some fellow that tells you to buy a specific pair, you will lose your clear and unbiased judgment and without even knowing, you will start to browse through the charts looking for trade setups that sustain that guy's theory and that have nothing to do with your trading system. It is your money; wouldn't you feel stupid if you would lose them by trading based on someone else's suggestions?

DON'T DO THIS

Now, after you finally construct your trading system according to all the rules above you must learn how to avoid making mistakes when putting your system to work.

PRICE PATTERN BREAKS

If your system includes trading price patterns, you must know that for a pattern to be considered broken price must close outside of it. If you have a trading system using price pattern breaks to signal your entry, then you must wait for a candle or bar to close outside the pattern on the same timeframe where you spotted the pattern.

Do not make the mistake to spot a pattern on the 4h chart

and then go the 15 minutes chart and wait for a 15 minutes candle to close outside and call this a break of the pattern. If the pattern resides on the 4h chart, you must always wait for a 4h candle to close outside with momentum, meaning that the candle should have at least half of its body outside the pattern to consider it a break. Let us see an example:

In the chart above, you have a descending triangle pattern. You can see that there is a candle that goes below the pattern but does not manage to close below the triangle at that first arrow there.

On the next candle, price quickly retraces back into the pattern. This is not a pattern break. On the second arrow there is indeed a candle closes strongly outside the pattern, with momentum; 3 quarters of its length are outside the pattern. This is a price pattern break. Even if the first candle that went outside the pattern would have closed at its low, that still would not have counted as a break because of the fact that it only went outside with less than half of its overall length.

If you are looking for a powerful trading system with price patterns and price action trends that can deliver more than 1000 pips per month you can check out my book Day Trading Forex with Price Patterns

CANDLESTICK CONFIRMATION

If your newly developed system uses candlestick patterns to confirm the trade entry you must always wait for that candlestick pattern to complete.

Wait for the last candle of the pattern to close before you enter the trade. If right at the close of the pattern there is some important economic news coming out they could invalidate your pattern and with it your entry signal. Remember that candlestick patterns work well because a lot of traders watch them and act on them. If you enter before the pattern completes and when the last candle finally closes you see that the pattern is not valid anymore then a lot of traders will not trade at that level because there is no valid pattern so you will be in the minority.

The minority always loses in forex. In addition, you have to know that candlestick patterns have their greatest success rate when found at price extremes. Let me show you what I mean:

All the patterns in the chart above are situated at extremes of price. There is no recent price action at that level preceding them. These kinds of candlestick patterns have a very high rate of success. If your confirmation pattern takes place at a level where price action is trading sideways it might not be a very good confirmation signal.

FIBONACCI RETRACEMENT LEVELS

If you use Fibonacci levels in your trading system, then always wait for the price to touch the level you are watching before you consider entering a trade. Do not trade if the price comes close to your Fibonacci retracement level but does not touch it.

Let me show you what I mean:

In the first attempt price comes close to the Fibonacci level but does not touch it.

It even makes a reversal candlestick pattern there suggesting that price will resume the trend down but soon after, price climbs back to the level this time touching and piercing it. This is the time to trade. If you had sold on the first attempt, you would have had your stop loss hit.

SUPPORT AND RESISTANCE

When trading with support and resistance levels make sure that you draw the most important ones, the pivotal ones where price bounces of them from either side.

These pivotal support and resistance zones are by far the most important ones they attract the most attention from the traders out there.

Do not beat yourself up with small, meaningless support and resistance zones. They are all over the place and they will clutter your charts for nothing.

Let me show you what a pivotal support or resistance zone

looks like:

You can see here that price coming from the upside bounces 4 times off of the support shown by the horizontal line in the middle of the chart there, finally goes below it, and then starts to bounce off of it coming from below on that last circle on the right.

The horizontal line is now acting as resistance after providing support for a long period of time, on multiple occasions.

These are very strong support and resistance zones that you always have to keep an eye on. They hold the test of time, when price comes towards them, either from above or below, it will react to it.

CUTTING PROFITS SHORT

This is a very common mistake made by novice traders. When a trade goes in your way for 100 pips do not close it in fear that price will come back to the entry level and eat all your profits.

Respect the trading system's rules and let the trade run until it hits your profit target or until it hits you stop loss level that you manually trailed above or below swings in the market.

You will never make money if you keep cutting your profits short because you fear of losing them. How would you feel if after you close the trade with 100 pips in profit, price goes on further and hits your target level at 200 pips in profit?

LETTING LOSSES RUN

This is also a very common mistake made by novice traders.

When you see that price is going towards your stop loss, don't ever move it further away thinking that it is just a spike in price and the trade will go your way eventually.

The second you remove that stop loss from its initial place decided by the system you constructed you put yourself under great risk.

Accept the small loss and wait patiently for the next trade setup. There will be some occasional loses; no system is perfect, just because you had a loss does not mean that you have to change the system because there is something wrong with it.

Accept the small drawdown and leave the stop loss level in its place otherwise, instead of a 20 pips loss, you will quickly find yourself in a position where you have no choice but to accept a much bigger loss.

It does not matter if you lose one trade, as you have seen earlier, you can be profitable even if you only win 33% of your trades with solid management rules.

REVENGE TRADING

If you lose one trade, keep calm, do not think to yourself that you have to recuperate the loss right away.

This is the worst thing you could do, to enter the market randomly and with a bigger order size, not obeying your trading system, thinking that you must get back the money you lost otherwise you won't sleep well through the night.

This is called revenge trading, and it clouds your judgment so hard that you could lose all your hard-earned money in a single day.

Close the computer and go about your business. Tomorrow is another day and you will get the money back surely if you trade according to your trading system.

50 PIPS A DAY FOREX STRATEGY

COMPONENTS

200 periods Exponential Moving Average

Support and Resistance levels

Candlesticks

This is a clean, easy to follow, and extremely profitable trading strategy to get you started in trading and to put you on the path of consistent profitability. It is better to trade with this strategy on the 4h chart but you can trade it on the daily as well.

The bigger the time frame the more important it is for the overall market movements, therefore, the more profitable your trading will be. It is very easy to understand and to put in practice immediately, anyone can do it if they know the basics of how the forex market works, what a forex pair is, and how to open and close an order.

I will now try to explain how each of the three components helps us to win trades with this strategy.

The moving average tells us what the main trend is on the 4h chart. This is very simple to do, just plot the 200 EMA on your 4h chart and observe where the current price is situated in respect to the moving average. If the pair at the current time trades above the moving average then the overall trend is up, if it trades below the moving average then the trend is down.

The moving average itself must have a clear slope in one direction. This means that for you to consider that the trend on the 4h chart is up the moving average must be sloping upwards and the pair has to be trading above it at that time. For a downtrend, the moving average must have a clear slope down and the pair has to trade below it.

This diagram shows exactly how to spot an uptrend.

After we establish that there is a clear trend we then move on to the next level and we will try to find a support or resistance level.

I have told you that the moving average helps us to gauge the trend on a pair. If we find a trend, we go on further analyzing that pair to find a support or a resistance level, where it is most likely that whoever is in charge of that pair (the buyers or the sellers), will pick up the pace, and resume the trend.

The support/resistance level has to be a diagonal one and the trend line drawn on the chart to construct it has to be sloping against the trend.

You draw this trend line on your chart by connecting at least two distinct points in the market although three points will be better. Here is what I mean:

In this diagram, you can see that after recognizing a clear downtrend we move forward to discover three resistance levels one after another.

On the first one (A) we draw a trend line to connect the three distinct swing lows found there, on the second one we have only two distinct points, and on the third one, we have four points to connect with a trend line.

The more points there are to connect the better, the more important the support/resistance is. You can also see that all these three levels are pointing up against the main trend, which is a requirement for this trading strategy.

These three levels at first served as support for price action but once they were broken to the downside, they turned into resistance levels.

Now, about the third component of this strategy.

This strategy uses candlesticks to enter trades. After finding a clear trend and a support or resistance zone, you have to wait for price to go back to that support/resistance level and retest it.

This is where the candlesticks come into play. Before you enter a trade in the direction of the main trend, there has to be a candlestick confirmation that the trend is indeed resuming.

You will be looking for big body candlesticks that close at or near the high or low, which shows that there is momentum in the market and the dominant side (buyers or sellers) have decided to step in and continue the trend.

Let me show you the same chart above again to see what I mean by retest of the resistance level:

You can see that each time the support was broken to the downside, it turned into resistance as price gets back up to retest/touch the trend line previously drawn. It will not always touch the trend line like in the examples above; sometimes it will get near it and then resume the trend without a touch.

This is also a retest. In the diagram above where we have a clear downtrend and resistance levels in place, we also have now retest movements. After this point we will be looking for big bearish candlesticks with big bodies and with no/small wick at the close to signify that the sellers have entered into the market again to push the price further down and extend the trend.

Let us look at the same chart again but this time focusing

on what happens after the retest.

This is the first resistance level out of those three. There is a touch of the resistance trend line made by that big bullish hollow/white candle. After this price makes 4 very small candles that tell us this level of price is a key level where buyers have a very hard time trying to push the price further up.

This type of candles represents indecision in the market, represents equilibrium. From the beginning of the retest, buyers had no problem pushing the price up which you can clearly see by those big consecutive bullish white candles. When price got to the resistance level, the situation changed. As the main trend was down, sellers were in control of this pair and they were just waiting for a more advantageous level to sell again and resume the downtrend. These advantageous levels are always situated at a support or resistance level. It can be horizontal support/resistance, it can be diagonal like the ones we are discussing, it can be a Fibonacci retracement level, which also acts as support and resistance, it can be the 200 period moving average on the daily chart or it can be a combination of some or all of the above.

The important thing to remember is that these are logical points in the market where buyers or sellers are most likely to step in and resume the main trend.

Okay, after those 4 small candles that tell us the buyers are losing their power, comes a big black bearish candle, much bigger than the preceding 4. This candle has a big body compared to the preceding candles and also closes near its low.

This candle is the footprint of the sellers coming into the market to push the price back down and resume the trend. The close of this candle is the level where you would have to sell this pair. When looking after big candles to enter the market after a retest of support/resistance it is important to always compare that candle with the preceding 2-3-4 candles. The entry candle always has to be bigger than the preceding ones, has to have a big body and close at or near the low if it is bearish or at or near its high if it is a bullish big candle that signifies the uptrend will resume.

You might think that I am exaggerating the importance of this entry candle. Well, to help you realize what it really means and why I say it is the footprint of the sellers coming into the market (in this downtrend example) you must think of these 4h candles from a time perspective. Before this big black candle in the example above there were three very small 4h candles that did not push the price up or down, it just traded there in a very small range.

When the big candle emerges, we see that the price pushed down and away from that small range. This signal candle is bigger than all of the preceding three combined and it was formed in 4 hours. The last three took 12 hours to form. This is what shows us the sellers have entered the market. In only 4 hours, they managed to move the price down more than they did in the last 12 hours. Let us see the second example:

In this second example, you can see that after the retest of the resistance trend line there are three bearish candles with decent body size, which would imply that sellers have stepped into the market again.

However, the first candle (A) of these three is preceded by a huge bullish white candle. This is not our signal to sell.

The second one(B) is bigger than the first and also has no big candles preceding it. However, you can see that it does not close at or near its low, it has a big wick there, price has retraced from the low of this candle and closed almost at its middle.

This does not give us the momentum we want when entering a trade. Finally, the third candle meets our requirements; therefore, we enter the short trade at the close of this candle.

This third example is a very interesting one because it brings up an important point about retest movements of support and resistance levels.

You see here that after price breaks the trend line to the downside, it comes back up very quickly to retest it, a trend line that has now turned into resistance, and then it makes a bearish black candle that could mean sellers have entered the market.

However, this is the 4h chart, this resistance line holds great significance, it took quite some time to develop, and a lot of 4h candles, the retest absolutely has to be bigger than two 4h candles. This is why you would have to disregard that first black candle as a signal to sell. It comes way too early; the retest has to be bigger two candles. If this would have been the 5 minutes or the 15 minutes chart, and the resistance level developed in 3 hours or so then yes, the retest could have been composed of just two candles.

Still, this is a very important resistance on the 4h chart that took days to develop; the retest will more than likely be bigger than two candles.

After this black candle, we see that there are additional candles that just stagnate around that area completing the retest of the resistance level.

Finally, we have a valid signal candle that indeed pushes the price way down(B).

STOP LOSS MANAGEMENT AND TAKE PROFIT LEVELS

Now that you know how and when to enter a trade let us discuss about where to set your stop loss levels, how to trail them manually, and how to determine your ideal take profit levels. The initial stop loss level that you set when entering the trade has to always be set at above or below the level where the retest of the support/resistance ends. After this, when price goes in your favor you trail manually your stop loss above or below every swing/turning point/minor support or resistance price makes. In addition to this, you will also be determining your take profit level before you actually enter into the trade.

This is very important from the money management perspective because there will be some rare occasions when after calculating your take profit and stop loss level before entering the trade you will find that the risk you will be taking with that trade is greater than the potential reward.

Otherwise said, you would have to risk losing more pips than you could potentially win with that particular trade. The risk-reward ratio in this case is not a satisfactory one.

When you find trades like this...DO NOT TRADE. Wait for the next opportunity. Money management makes you profitable in the long run; always keep this in mind. Be very disciplined when analyzing charts and entering trades.

Always treat trading as a business and not as a game. Let us see an example of how to manage the stop loss and take profit levels.

This is that first resistance level we talked about. Before entering the trade at the close of the signal black candle, you predetermine your take profit level in the following way: join with a trend line two points, the first swing of the resistance trend line and the point where the retest movement started.

The first swing of the resistance is the upper circle in this chart and the start of the retest is the second circle.

After this, extend this trend line down, and where the future price action will touch it, that is your take profit and the level where you exit the trade.

The stop loss will be set initially where the retest finished like shown in this chart and after this, as price progresses down it gives you logical turning points in the market where you can trail the stop loss (SL2).

Also in this example, you can see before entering the trade that the risk is far less than the reward. This was a 420 pips winning trade.

In this second example, the trend line for the take profit level extends far out of reach for the current price but, as long as the reward is greater than the risk(and it is), you will have no problem in entering the trade and trailing your stop loss above every turning point until it finally gets hit.

This trade actually went more in favor than this chart can illustrate and managed 550 pips of profit.

This is the example with that small retest. Before entering the trade, you draw the trend line to find out where your potential take profit will be and you see that you would have to exit the trade before you even enter it which is of course non-sense.

In addition, if that trend line would have been 10 pips lower and you would have had the chance to enter the trade, this was still not a good trade because the risk would have been greater than the 10 pips reward. Stay out of trades like this one.

There will be plenty of opportunities, this kind of trades happen frequently. An alternative way to predetermine your take profit level when the first method renders the trade unsatisfactory because of the high risk and low reward is the following:

Connect with a trend line the last minor swing the pair made before the trend line(A) was broken to the downside (in the case of a downtrend) and the same start of the retest move(D circle).

Use whichever method gives you a better take profit level as long as it is not exaggerated and you think there are extremely low chances that the market will actually go to that level. If this method also does not help you achieve a good risk-reward ratio, then ignore the trade completely.

A second method that you can use to take advantage of the fact that every support becomes a resistance and every resistance becomes a support level after they have been broken it to use the same rules as with the method above, but applying them to horizontal support and resistance zones this time. However, with the diagonal support and resistance zones you have seen that they are formed by connecting two or more distinct swings in the market. With the horizontal levels, often times, you will not have a second distinct swing that you can use to draw a horizontal line. Knowing this, you must leave the candlestick chart and go to the same 4-hours chart, but a bar chart this time, and zoom it out completely.

Let me show you an example of this.

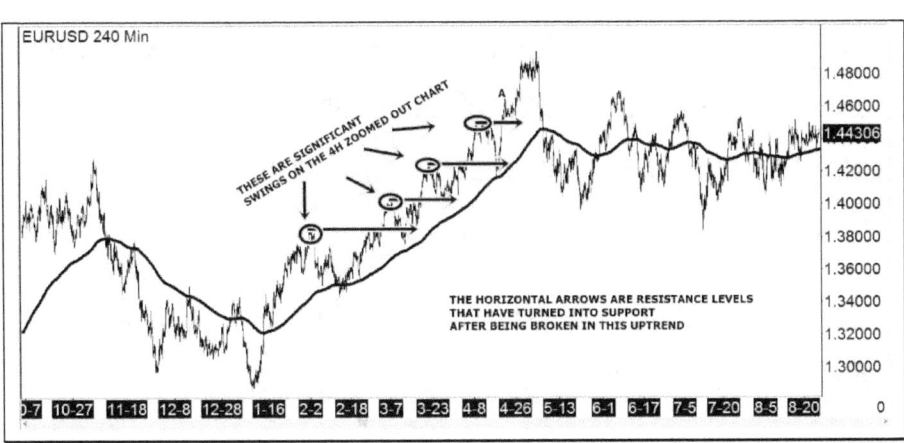

Please note that these horizontal levels come into existence just by drawing an extended horizontal line at the level where the important swings in the market are. If you want to trade the retest of these levels successfully, you have to make sure initially that they hold great importance to the overall movements of your particular forex pair. A way to make sure of this is by zooming out completely the chart like in the example above to see the big picture of the price action movements.

This way, you can put your support or resistance level into context, you can judge by looking at the surrounding price action if a swing is indeed important or not.

For example, in the chart above, after the last horizontal level, there is a minor swing that price has made there(A). You can see that I have not considered it as I think that this swing is smaller than the preceding ones on this pair and it does not hold great significance to the overall context of this pair.

Size of the swings matters. The small one is important on a lower timeframe, not on the 4 hours.

After you identify these meaningful horizontal levels, you will have no problem trading a retest of them, exactly like in the method above with the diagonal support and resistance areas. Let us see an example:

As you can see, things are clear in this trade example. The moving average is sloping up and the pair is trading above it. There is a clear uptrend.

You zoom out the chart and you find that this swing is actually quite significant by looking at the big picture.

You draw the extended horizontal line and you go back to the candlestick zoomed in chart to wait for the retest to take place(which is what this chart is showing).

The retest does indeed happen right at the horizontal support level and soon enough, you have a confirmation that the buyers have entered into the market again at this level and they are most likely to push the price upwards and extend the uptrend.

The confirmation is represented by that big, white, bullish candle that is also your signal candle to enter a buy order. The buy order is opened at the close of the signal candle of course. Trade management (stop loss and take profit) is made exactly like with the diagonal levels method.

PRICE ACTION BREAKDOWN AND IN DEPTH GUIDE TO PRICE ACTION TRADING ARE THE LATEST BOOKS THAT I HAVE WRITTEN. THEY ARE VERY POPULAR, CONSTANTLY BEING IN THE TOP 10 ON AMAZON, IN THEIR CATEGORY. PRICE ACTION BREAKDOWN WAS NUMBER ONE ON ITS CATEGORY FOR A YEAR WHEN IT WAS AVAILABLE TO READERS WHO SUBSCRIBE TO THE KINDLE UNLIMITED PROGRAM. EVEN AFTER GOING OUT OF KINDLE UNLIMITED, STILL MANAGES TO GO TO NUMBER ONE FROM TIME TO TIME.

IN AN EFFORT TO PERSUADE YOU TO EXPRESS YOUR OPINION ABOUT THE BOOK/BOOKS PUBLICLY SO THAT OTHER READERS CAN MAKE MORE INFORMED PURCHASING DECISIONS, I WOULD LIKE TO MAKE THE FOLLOWING PROPOSAL : IF YOU DO PURCHASE THE KINDLE VERSION OF ONE OR BOTH OF MY LATEST BOOKS MENTIONED ABOVE, I WOULD KINDLY ASK YOU TO REVIEW THEM ON AMAZON AFTER READING. IN EXCHANGE FOR YOU TAKING THE TIME TO WRITE A REVIEW WITH YOUR OPINION ABOUT THE BOOK/BOOKS, I WOULD LIKE TO MAKE AN OFFER.

FOR ONE VERIFIED PURCHASE REVIEW YOU WRITE ON ANY OF THE 2 BOOKS ABOVE, I CAN OFFER THE PDF VERSION OF THE REVIEWED BOOK, THE PDF VERSION OF THIS BOOK YOU ARE CURRENTLY READING, PLUS ONE OTHER BOOK OF MINE (ALSO IN PDF VERSION), AT YOUR CHOOSING, FROM THE ONES I WROTE IN 2012 (THIS INCLUDES ALL BUT THE TWO IN QUESTION).

IF YOU DECIDE TO FOLLOW THROUGH ON THIS OFFER, AFTER THE REVIEW HAS BEEN COMPLETED, PLEASE EMAIL ME AT LAURENTIUDAMIR@GMAIL.COM, SPECIFY ON WHAT AMAZON WEBSITE HAS THE REVIEW BEEN POSTED, UNDER WHAT USER NAME AND WHAT OTHER BOOK OF MINE WOULD YOU LIKE TO RECEIVE IN PDF FORMAT, BESIDES THE REVIEWED ONE AND THE ONE YOU ARE CURRENTLY READING

In the end I would like to apologize if I sound a little rigid in my explanations and if there are any misspellings. English is not my first language. I am doing the best I can.

If you find that this adds value to your trading please consider writing a review of the book on Amazon. It does not have to be long, just a few words to state your opinion about the trading system presented in order to help other people make more informed decisions.

Thank you for reading this book and happy forex trading. Hope you found it valuable.

DAY TRADING FOREX WITH S&R ZONES STRATEGY

TABLE OF CONTENTS

INTRODUCTION

Day trading the foreign exchange market can be very profitable if you know what you are doing, if you have a set of rules to follow and if you have the discipline and patience to respect them. Let me show you what this day trading system can do if applied to the forex market:

You can see in the diagram above two trades taken using this system. All the trades with this forex strategy look exactly the same. They have small stop loss levels and a high reward. The first sell order in the example above won 210 pips, the second sell order made 250 pips.

Here is another trade example with this strategy. Very small stop loss, 215 pips profit. I will now go through every component of this trading strategy, explain them in detail and at the end, put them together to give you the complete forex trading system.

MOVING AVERAGE

This system uses the 200 period exponential moving average or 200EMA. You have to insert this moving average on your charts because it will tell you if you have to look for trade setups to buy or look for trade setups to sell. This is the most popular moving average in the trading markets; many people watch it and use it as a direction indicator.

This strategy uses this moving average in the following way: when the price of any forex pair is completely above the moving average we start looking for trade setups to only buy the pair. When the pair is trading completely below this moving average, we will be looking for trade setups only to sell that pair.

Let me show you more clearly what this means:

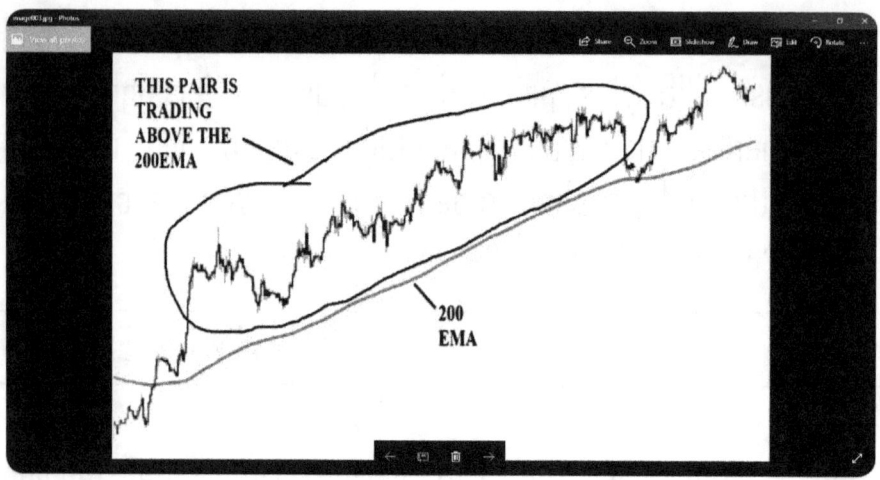

As you can see in the diagram above, price action for this pair is completely above the exponential moving average, it never touches it. This is good; it means that you can start to look for trade setups. We will do that later.

If the price does touch the 200EMA but quickly bounces back up like it did in the chart above at the end there, that is also a good thing. Now let me show you when not to look for trade setups even if the price is above or below the moving average:

Here you can see that price is above the moving average for the most part but it intersects with it there in the middle of the chart and does not bounce back up quickly enough. The pair trades there in the zone of the EMA, passing it multiple times, returning to the upside, and then crossing it again to the downside.

This is not good; it means that the uptrend in this case, is not strong enough so you will not be looking for trade setups if you see this kind of price action behavior. You always have to look for the price action to be completely above or below the moving average or just touching it for a brief period and then bounce off of it and resume its direction.

There is one more important thing about the moving

average that you always have to keep an eye on. The slope of the moving average has to be always in the direction of the price action. In the two charts above you can see that the direction of the price action is clearly to the upside and so is the slope of the moving average, it's pointing up. On the last chart, in that middle section that we discussed you can see that the moving average has no slope there, it is sideways. That is a good indication to stay out of the market. Let me give you an example:

When you see this on one of your charts, you have to go visit some other pair to look for trade setups. The moving average is almost horizontal, and the price action is ranging, it's going up and down crossing the EMA.

TIMEFRAMES

We will be using the 4 hours timeframe to see the overall trend as explained earlier. If the pair trades above the 200 period exponential moving average then the trend is up, if it trades below the moving average then the trend is down. After we do this, we go to the 1 hour chart and do the same thing. If on the 4h chart price is above the EMA, on the 1 hour chart price must also be above the moving average for us to consider looking for trade setups on that pair.

Same goes for the other direction, if on the 4h chart the pair is trading below the EMA, on the 1h chart price must also be trading below the 200EMA and the EMA itself must be sloping down on both timeframes.

Only when these conditions are met we will watch that pair for potential trades and only in the direction of the trend shown to us by the 200EMA. If a pair is trading above the moving average on the 4h and 1h charts and the EMA is sloping up on both charts then we will be looking for trade setups to buy that pair.

If a pair is trading below the moving average on both 4h and 1h charts and the EMA is sloping down on both timeframes we will be looking to sell that pair if a trade setup occurs.

You might ask yourself why do you need to look at the same moving average on two different timeframes. Well, the answer is - confirmation. If on the 4h chart, the pair trades above the EMA this tells us that the overall trend of that pair is up.

When you go to the 1h chart and see that the same thing is happening there too, then you have a confirmation of what you saw on the 4h chart and you also know that the overall trend is gaining strength and momentum because the short term trend on the 1h chart is in line with the bigger trend.

These are the perfect conditions for you to trade and maximize your profits. When these conditions present themselves on a chart then you will be using the same 1h chart zoomed out to find the most significant support or resistance area.

After identifying these areas, you will stay on the same 1h chart but zoomed in this time to wait for a trade setup to occur and then carry the trade from entry to exit. We will discuss how to do this later.

You may ask yourself why to trade on the 1h chart and not the 5 or 15 minutes chart. Day trading is not about entering trades on the smallest timeframe possible. The smaller the timeframe the less accurate your trading setups will be and the more losing trades you will have.

For a trade setup to be a winner it must hold significance within the overall picture. A support or resistance level on the zoomed out 1h chart has far greater importance than one on a smaller timeframe, therefore it has much greater chances of success.

SUPPORT AND RESISTANCE

As I said earlier, we will be looking for significant support or resistance levels on the zoomed out 1h chart. Here is a chart to show you what to look for:

In the above 1h chart, you can see that there is a downtrend, price is below the 200EMA, and the moving average is sloping down.

The same is true for the 4h chart on that pair at that moment in time. You can see three points in the market where buyers have stepped up to push the price up only for the seller to step in again and resume the downtrend surpassing these levels. Those three levels are support zones.

In the chart above you can see the short-term trend in up and the moving average is sloping up.

The same thing is happening on the 4h chart for that same period of time. Sellers try to push the price down and this creates those 4 turning points in the market that become resistance levels, which the buyers will have to overcome by pushing the price back up in the initial direction and resuming the uptrend. A very important notion that you have to know in order to identify these support and resistance levels correctly is the degree.

You can see in the above two charts that there are many more support and resistance levels on them but I only marked 3 of them on the first chart and 4 of them on the second. The reason for this is that a support or resistance level is significant only if it has the same degree or the same amplitude as the rest of them. Let me show you the last chart again:

This is the same chart as the last one. You can see that apart from the four important resistance levels, we also have two minor resistance levels that are very small; therefore, they hold no real importance to the overall trend.

We do not consider those small turning points as resistance levels, instead we wait for a resistance to form with approximately the same size or amplitude as the preceding ones. Let us look again now at the first chart in this chapter:

Here too we had a very small support just after the first real big support.

Now, you know anything there is to know about the moving average on the two timeframes, you know exactly what market conditions to look for with respect to this moving average and you also know how to spot significant support and resistance zones on the zoomed out 1h chart.

What this system does is to wait for a break of these support/resistance levels once the market is presenting you a clear direction of the trend, direction that you will gauge with the 200EMA as described in the moving average section.

A break of an important support or resistance level occurs

when a 1h candle closes below the support or above the resistance with more than half of its body. Let us see an example:

You can see in this diagram that the breakout 1h candle closes below the support level and more than half of its body is situated below the support level.

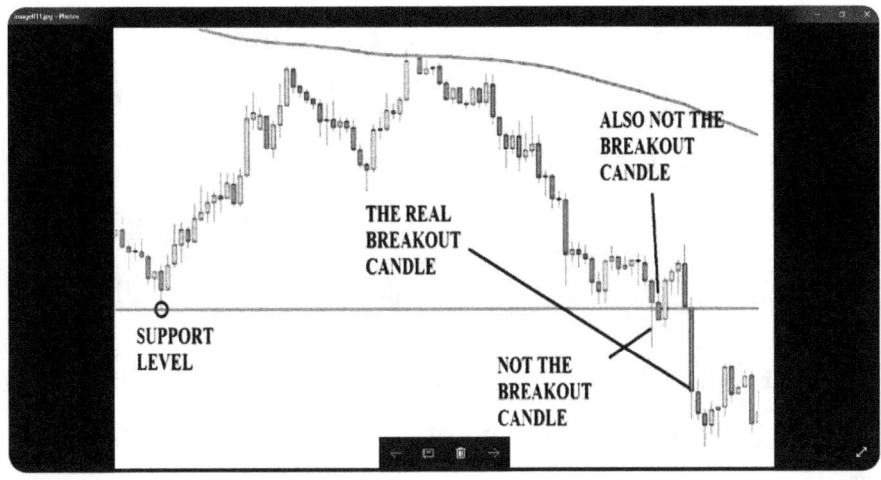

In the example above, we have something very interesting. The first candle that tries to break through the support level fails and quickly goes back up closing within the territory of the support level. This is definitely not the breakout candle. Next, we have a small candle that indeed closes below the support area and also has more than half of its body below the support.

This corresponds to the definition of the breakout I gave earlier but there is a problem with this candle: It is very small in size. Do not consider such small candles as breakout candles even if they fit the definition of a breakout. For a breakout to be true, it has to happen with force, price has to create a big candle to show us that the sellers in this case, are committed to push the price down further. A small candle does not show too much commitment from the sellers. Such small candles usually form in late New York session and in the Asian session when the market in choppy and there is not much volume in the market. A valid strong breakout usually takes place in the European session.

Next, we finally have a breakout of that support level with a huge bearish candle that is entirely below the support level. This is the true breakout and this is what we will use to enter our orders in the market.

ENTRY

You probably know that almost every time a strong support or resistance level is broken price comes back to retest it shortly after. This retest is what you will use to find the entry level for your order and also your stop loss level.

After the breakout candle closes price will come back to the support or resistance level and retest it before continuing in the direction of the breakout. After you see that price has retested the level you enter a pending stop order at the point where the retest began and after your order gets filled you set your stop loss level at the point where the retest finished. Let us see a chart to explain this better:

In this example we have the price below the moving average on both 1h and 4h charts and the EMA is sloping down on the two timeframes. We have a breakout of the strong support level previously marked by us. After the breakout candle price goes a little further down and then starts to climb back up to retest the support level represented here by the red horizontal line.

This is the point where we set our sell stop order. Price retests the level and stays there for a while before it comes back down to resume the downtrend and triggers our sell order. When our order gets triggered we know that the retest has finished and price is resuming the trend in the direction of the breakout so we set our stop loss level just above the point where the retest move has finished as show in the chart. Let us see another example:

The same thing is happening here also. A breakout of the support with a strong candle, a retest, and then a selloff.

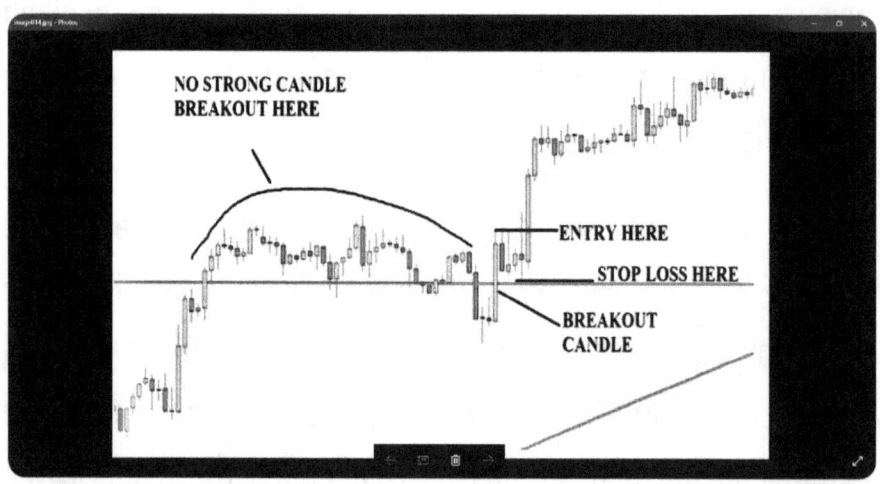

This example is very interesting as price goes above the strong resistance but there is no strong convincing breakout candle. Price just trades above the resistance level but it does not give us strong clues that the buyers have stepped in to resume the uptrend. Only later, we see that we have a strong bullish candle away from the resistance and very shortly after, we have a retest and then price shoots up. This is our trade setup as shown in the chart.

	EXIT

To exit the trades you have to use something that lets you exit just at the moment when the trend is ending and price starts to go against you and eat into your hard-earned profits.

The best tool for doing this is a price pattern and it is called the wedge pattern. The wedge pattern can be, depending on its location, a continuation pattern, and a reversal pattern. As we seek a way to signal us when a trend in about to end we will use it only as a reversal pattern. Let me give you an example to see how this pattern looks like:

The wedge pattern consists of two lines that converge at the end. These lines are formed by connecting the most recent swing highs and the most recent swing lows as in the chart above.

When this pattern emerges it almost always means that the trend is in its final moments. Therefore, when we have a trade opened and we are in profit, we look at the chart to see if there is such a pattern by connecting the last two minor highs and the last two minor lows that price makes on the zoomed out candlestick 1h chart. Let me show you know where exactly you exit the trade after discovering this price pattern:

This way you will rarely have a trade that goes against you and eat your profits because you did not exit when you were supposed to.

In 90% of cases, these reversal patterns do form at the end of the trends, but if you cannot find this pattern from time to time when trading, you will then use the moving average to exit the trade. When selling, if there is no wedge pattern you exit the trade when a 1h candle closes above the 200EMA, when buying, exit when a candle closes below the moving average like in the example below:

In these cases when there is no wedge pattern, you can also use a simple trend line to connect the highs if you are selling or the lows if you are buying. If there is no wedge, draw the trend line and when it is broken by a 1h candle closing above or below it then exit the trade.

You bought this pair above but there is no wedge pattern.

There is however, a trend line that you can draw by connecting all the lows that price makes, when going up in profit. Exit when the trend line breaks. Notice that the moving average is way down, the trend line always gives you a much better exit level.

So, when exiting a trade you must first look for a wedge, in the majority of cases you will find one, but if you don't then draw a trend line. If you cannot draw a trend either then use the moving average break to exit the trade.

To conclude this trading system let's recap what you should do:

Plot the 200 EMA on your chart.

Look at the 4h chart and see if the pair is trading above or below the moving average and if the slope of this moving average is up or down.

Do the same on the 1h zoomed out chart, if things look exactly the same like on the 4h chart then mark the most recent strong support or resistance level an trade the break of it like shown in the sections above. If market conditions do not coincide on the two timeframes of the same pair than you have no trade there, go to the following pair. Let's see a trade example:

We have a breakout of the support here, we enter the trade, we set the stop loss, price trades in a small range for a while, and then it goes strongly in our favor. Let's see what happens next:

This was a 400 pip winning trade.

TAKE PROFIT LEVEL DETERMINATION

Now that you know how to exit the trades it is time for you to find out how to use price action to predetermine you take profit level. When you first enter the trade, the system gives you a stop loss level and now it will give you an initial take profit level as well.

This TP level will not be set in the market because it is not a fixed value; it depends on the speed of the price movements and their direction. Ideally, price will touch it easily and you will not have to worry about a thing but if the price does not go to this take profit level and instead makes a reversal wedge or breaches the trend line or the moving average then you exit the trade manually as explained earlier. After you enter the trade and put your stop loss in place you must do the following: on the zoomed out 1hour chart you connect with a trend line the current support or resistance level (the one that you are trading the break of) with the previous one like in the chart below:

You can see in this chart that after entering the buy order at the break of that resistance and after putting your stop loss in place you should draw a trend line(the red line in the chart) to connect that resistance level with the previous one and then extend it forward like in this example. When price goes in your favor, it will start to approach your trend line. When it finally touches it you exit the trade, the touch of the trend line is your take profit. Here is an example of a short trade:

This is it. In the end I would like to apologize if I sound a little to rigid in my explanations and if there are any misspellings.English is not my first language. I am doing the best I can.

If you find that this adds value to your trading please consider writing a review of the book on Amazon. It does not have to be long, just a few words to state your opinion about the trading system presented in order to help other people make more informed decisions.